Daughter Arise

John Das

Published by Das Publishing
Daughter Arise
John Das
P.O.Box: 1020 Pineville, NC 28134, USA
Email: DaughterAriseBook@gmail.com

ISBNs
Kenyan Edition (5.25" x 8") – 978-1-965959-03-9
US Paperback (6" x 9") – 978-1-965959-01-5
US Hardcover (6" x 9") – 978-1-965959-00-8
eBook (Global) – 978-1-965959-02-2

First Published 2025

DAS PUBLISHING

EST 2025

About the Book

Daughter Arise is a powerful exploration of resilience, empowerment, and transformation. Written to inspire women from all walks of life, this book delves into the challenges, triumphs, and profound moments that shape us. It is a heartfelt call to action, encouraging every woman to rise above life's obstacles and embrace her unique strength and purpose.

Filled with heartfelt stories, practical wisdom, and empowering insights, Daughter Arise is a guide for overcoming adversity and stepping into your full potential. This book aims to motivate, heal, and encourage readers to take bold steps toward a fulfilling and meaningful life.

With authenticity and compassion, Daughter Arise celebrates the courage and resilience of women. It is a reminder of the extraordinary power within each of us to overcome, transform, and thrive.

About the Author

John Das is a passionate community leader. He and his wife Roslyn lead with a heart of compassion to bring healing to others. He is the founder and executive director of Daughter Arise, which is much more than a book. Daughter Arise is a movement designed to help women from every walk of life to arise. John and Roslyn have been married for over 25 years and have five wonderful children: Isaac, Michael, Jasmine, Justine, and Julia. John was born in America and grew up in Virginia and Kenya.

John is also an author and advocate. This book, Daughter Arise, aims at empowering women to step out of the shadows and embrace life. Drawing from his experience as a husband, father to daughters, and pastor, as well as his close relationship with his mother, John shares profound insights. John's book and outreach to others are inspired by years of hearing heart-wrenching stories of trafficking, abuse, and oppression during conversations he has had with women from all over the world, which left an indelible burden on his heart. Together with his wife, Roslyn, they have provided refuge for trafficked women, creating a safe haven for those in danger.

"Why now?" John Das explains, "This book has been on my heart for over 15 years, and Daughter Arise will be the first of several books I hope to write to help people around the world."

In addition to his global ministry, which spans Africa, Europe, Asia, and the Americas, John Das has initiated impactful movements like Students for Christ International, Redemption Development Corporation, Youth Restoration Inc., East Coast Revival Ministry, and Revive Church, currently in Charlotte and Houston. His church ministry is marked by powerful teaching, prophetic worship, and creative expressions such as music and drama, all aimed at bringing hope, healing, revival, and restoration. Today John Das continues to inspire and uplift countless lives, fulfilling his mission to ignite faith and transformation in all he reaches out to.

Does God Really Care About Me?

Does God really love me? Does He really care? Is it possible that God made a mistake with my life and my very existence? If God never makes mistakes, why does life feel so unfair? Why do I keep facing pain and challenges?

These are questions that many people around the world continue to ask every day. As you read this book, we will delve into these queries and more. God has a perfect plan for all of us, but what God intended, Satan has deliberately disrupted by using us, humanity, to do it. Intentionally or unintentionally, some of us, at some point, through our actions and decisions, have partnered with Satan to cause pain to others, therefore, disrupting, dismantling, or even destroying the beautiful things God created. One of those things is the male and female relationship, and what it was supposed to be.

What has plagued women for centuries still happens today. God's daughters are constantly treated as less than who He intended them to be. Right now, as you read these words, God's daughters are being raped, molested, abused, misused, trafficked, terrorized, traumatized, marginalized, and murdered. If you have participated in the demoralization of women in any way, whether you are male or female, you have partnered with the enemy by consorting and colluding in the condemnation of one of God's greatest and most precious creations, The Woman.

What we are facing today regarding the mistreatment of women across the world began in the Garden of Eden a long time ago. This began when a man, the first man, abandoned his responsibility and chose not to cover the gift he was given. It was initiated when the man decided to blame the woman rather than be accountable and repent on behalf of himself and his family.It all began when the enemy planted seeds of doubt in the heart of the first woman, Eve.. She felt that God, her father, designer, and creator, did not trust her, and that her husband did not stand up for her during her greatest time of need, causing everything to be shattered. So how do we solve this? How do we fix it? What do we do? Where do we go from here?

Keep reading to find out.

Foreword

John Das is a passionate leader committed to seeing women live out their full potential in the kingdom of God. This book, Daughter Arise, offers more than a good read. Daughter Arise is a movement.

It is a title. It is a command.

It intertwines the accounts of biblical women who speak to women of the twenty-first century and beyond. Daughter Arise calls the souls of women to elevate transformatively. This movement affects women and seeks to empower and equip society regardless of age, gender, culture, or ethnicity.

We say yes to the mandate. We will arise. We will prayerfully move forth with a restorative, resurrective, and redemptive mindset. Let's go. Arise!

Dr. Barbara L. Peacock

Acknowledgements

To my beloved wife, Roslyn, your unwavering support and love have been my foundation throughout this journey. Thank you for standing beside me, believing in my vision, and making countless sacrifices along the way. Your presence is a priceless gift in my life.

To my wonderful daughters, Jasmine, Justine, and Julia, you are my greatest treasures. Watching you grow into the extraordinary young women you have become today fills my heart with immense joy. Your love, laughter, and encouragement inspire me more than words can express.

To my cherished mother, your unwavering faith and belief in God have been the bedrock of everything that you do. Your love and sacrifices have helped to shape who I am, and I am endlessly thankful for you.

And to my mother-in-law, your wisdom and advice have been a steady source of strength and hope. Your prayers and care for me and our family mean more to me than you know.

This book is a testament to the remarkable women in my life. Thank you for being my anchor, my inspiration, and my greatest cheerleader.

Six amazing ladies in my life. My wife, my mom, my mother-in-law, and my three daughters.

Dedication

This book is dedicated to the fearless women who rise against all odds, to those who face life's challenges with grace and courage, and to those who inspire others through their resilience. May this work honor you and encourage countless others to embrace their power and purpose.

Testimonial

People claim countlessly how books can change your perspective and change your life. As an avid reader, I must say this is not always true. When given the task to be one of the first to read this book, I thank God that I was alone while reading it. Several times I could barely see through the tears in my eyes. I didn't see the Apostle John Das. I saw God. I felt God. I felt the saving grace and anointing of Jesus Christ right through these pages! I felt heard. I felt loved. I felt seen!

I had a moment when I removed the words from in front of me, and I just cried. Not tears of pain or anguish. Let me explain. Have you ever argued with someone, and no matter how much you tried, you just felt like they just didn't get it? As a woman, I must say, I've felt that more than I'd like to admit. I am either too sensitive. Too emotional. Too irrational. Too complicated. Just too much. Then it's that rare moment when you are speaking to someone and they match every complex thought in your mind that you gave up on trying to get others to understand because it just wasn't worth the fight anymore. My tears were laced with a moment of, "Oh…the creation of me was very intentional, not a mistake…just misused."

Daughter Arise ushers you into a very private, intimate moment with God that is unmatched, exposing, and full of raw emotions. As you enter into this journey, I encourage you to read this book in your isolated space, a place where you already have your one-on-one time with God. If you don't have one, create it. You will want to be alone without distractions. Speaking from experience, I appreciated the spiritual space I entered into as I reflected on my past, my present, and my future walk with Christ.

I commend Apostle John Das and Pastor Roslyn Das for leading a life that allows them to be so aware of God's daughters.

It is time to arise.

Shauntie Johnson

CONTENTS

Introduction

Daughter Arise is personified by the story of Esther, who went from being an orphan to becoming a queen. She overcame every obstacle in her path to be all God intended her to be. When it was time for her to arise, she did, despite the enemy's plan to destroy her and the people she loved. Like Esther, we believe God has a great plan for your life.

Each one of us is specially and wonderfully made by him. God has given all of us gifts and talents to bless others, glorify him, and even enhance our own lives, but, like Esther, even with the most incredible gifts, talents, and abilities, we all need help to arise.

Consider these scriptures about God giving us the power we need to arise. John 10:10 declares, "The thief has only come to steal and to kill and to destroy, but I have come that they may have life and have it more abundantly." And John 11:21-25, announces," Now Martha said to Jesus, 'Lord, if you had been here, my brother would not have died." Jesus said to her, your brother will rise again." Martha said to him, "I know that on the last day, He will rise again in the resurrection," but Jesus said to her, "I am the resurrection and the life. He who believes in Me, though he were dead, yet shall he live.""

Have you lost something along the way? Do you feel stuck, tired, or hopeless often or sometimes? Jesus Christ has come to give you life no matter what you've gone through or what you're currently going through. God can resurrect and restore every dead or dying thing in your life by the power of our risen lord and savior, Jesus Christ.

Daughter Arise wants to bring life to you. We want to help you accomplish your purpose and fulfill your destiny. We want to help women arise. In the pages of this book, we can say confidently, that you will experience being a daughter of the most high God, and experience the prolific words of Jesus, "Daughter, arise."

Like Jarius' daughter, you are not dead. You are not deceased. You are not a corpse. You are alive. Jesus declares the little girl was only sleeping. Like Jesus, we intend to put everything and everyone around you who is mourning your life, your dreams, or your existence out of the room, out of your mind, and out of your life. Like Jesus, we declare you are not dead; you are only sleeping, and we fully intend to see the hand of God lifting you out of your spiritual or emotional grave. It's time to arise!

Your salvation has already been paid for. Your ability to arise first came when Jesus Christ arose from the grave. The hard part has already been done. But if you don't know it, can't see or find it, then you'll continue to feel lost and hopeless even though you have a father in heaven who loves and cares for you very much.

God has a special, unique plan for your life. Hear the decree of Jeremiah 29:11, "For I know the plans I have for you, declares the Lord, plans to prosper you and not to harm you, plans to give you hope and a future." Daughter, arise!

Chapter One: *I'm Sorry*

I have been married for over 25 years. During that time, like many of my male counterparts, I've had to apologize many times. But over time, I have learned how to apologize effectively and sincerely. Most importantly, I've learned that real apologies do matter. An apology should be sincere. More so, an apology accompanied by acts of love and kindness, along with real change, truly makes a difference.

As a man who has in the past caused pain, I can truly say, "I'm sorry." I am sorry for whatever you went through in your life that brought you hurt, sorrow, and sadness. As a seasoned pastor, who has been in ministry for over 30 years, the apology I give today comes with an act of love and kindness by writing this book. Let me say it again—I am truly sorry for everything you've gone through in your life and that has brought you pain, sorrow, suffering, tears, setbacks, and shame. I am sorry.

Yet, this chapter isn't just about me saying sorry. It's about someone else who asked me to apologize to you on their behalf. You may ask who this person is and what they have done. This person loves you very much. He cares about you more than you could ever imagine. He created you. He has a unique purpose and a plan for your life. That's right. I'm talking about God.

You may not believe it, but God had a conversation with me, and He wanted me to tell you He's sorry. You're probably wondering why God would say He's sorry and why He would use a man to do so. The terrible things that happened to you were never God's will. He's sorry mankind made the decision to deviate from His plan for all of us. He's apologizing for how men in general have distorted His pure and perfect will for you. He's sorry about the rape, molestation, misuse, abuse, divorce, disregard, and belittlement you have experienced. He's sorry you've been treated like a second-class citizen. He's sorry you've been trafficked, pimped, and put on a pole. He's sorry you were denied entrance into boardrooms and offices you worked hard for and that were rightfully yours.

God is sorry you were treated as if you were stupid, incompetent, or slow. He's sorry you weren't paid what you deserved, when you weren't promoted yet you worked hard, when you were used and expected to accept being used and abused with a smile. He's sorry you were made to act like everything was okay in public while being beaten in private. He's sorry you worked like an animal and were treated as property. He's sorry you were made to feel not good enough, beautiful enough, smart enough, sexy enough, or even religious enough. He's sorry you became a part of someone else's sinful decision.

I know you might be wondering, if God were really sorry, why would He allow what happened to you? Couldn't He have stopped my rapist? Couldn't He have intervened in my molestation? If God were really sorry, then why did he allow it to happen in the first place? I do believe there are answers to help us, men and women alike, on this sometimes tiresome and treacherous journey called life.

There is an age-old question out there. Why do bad things happen to good people? If God loves and cares about us, why do we go through bad or difficult things? Calamity, pain, death, destruction, abandonment, or loneliness were never a part of the formula for God's creation. Those evil, wicked, and torturous things many go through were never a part of the plan or the will of God for our lives. So why do they still happen? And why doesn't God stop all of them?

Here's my take on it. In the beginning, God created the heavens and the earth. He then designed everything, an environment, along with plants and creatures, and we were given dominion over all of it. Dominion means power, authority, and control. It also means responsibility. In its purest form, dominion simply means to take something that someone has ownership and control over and place that thing into the ownership and control of someone else.

That was the plan. The plan was for men and women to live in harmony. There was no division, schism, or conflict between men and women in God's initial plan. The earth and everything on it was given to mankind, not just to steward, but to own and have control over. While the plan has not changed, the expected outcome did, because of sin. God can never lie, nor would God forage or steal. The authority and dominion given to mankind, God did not rescind.

The evil we see on earth is not God's doing. It's all man's fault. Period! The wickedness we see in this world is because of what mankind chose to do. All sin is a choice. We cannot have the luxury of sin and then somehow escape or avoid the penalty for it. Every choice has a consequence. Every action has a reaction, and unfortunately, sin affects the innocent, as well as the guilty.

Consider Cain & Abel. Cain had a choice. He chose to kill his brother. That is how he handled his dominion. It is how he handled his authority. God didn't instruct Cain to kill Abel. God gave Cain the authority to choose. If you choose to do the right thing, the results are usually good (positive, productive, or beneficial). If you choose to do the wrong thing, the results are usually bad (negative, harmful, or destructive).

So, what is God so sorry about? He's sorry you were the recipient of someone else's wicked choice. He's sorry someone decided to use their power in a sinful way to assault you and take away your power as if it were theirs to take. He's sorry a man or another woman chose to mishandle their dominion and disrespect yours. He's sorry that the authority given to mankind was used to belittle, disparage, insult, and injure you. It was never His intention to see what He gave us all in love exploited and mismanaged. While the plan was for mankind to have power, authority, and dominion, it was never designed to make you feel less than the beautiful and valuable person God created you to be.

In this deep, dark, and complicated matter, God has asked me to represent Him. He has asked me to be His mouthpiece on this earth, and to do my best to explain to women that He is sorry for what has happened to them, especially in the hands of men. So, bear with me as I do my best to communicate the heart of God through my human mind and limited understanding of the hearts, minds, feelings, emotions, pain, suffering, trauma, and debilitating memories of His precious daughters.

Why an Apology is Needed

(In the words of God…) I did this. I decided it was not good for "man" to be alone. Adam had nothing to do with it. He didn't ask for it. It wasn't his choice. It was mine. I didn't want him to choose something wrong, so I made the choice for him. I chose "woman" because that was what I wanted for him. I wanted someone who would help him, walk beside him, speak his language, and connect with him spiritually, emotionally, and physically. So, I put him to sleep and gave Adam a woman. He had no say in the matter.

I took his rib, not a part from his head or his feet. This helper wasn't going to be above him, or beneath him. I took a bone right from the middle. I took a rib. Ribs help to cover and protect vital organs, especially the heart. I could have done it any other way. I am God. But I chose to do it this way. I could have created you from the dirt like I did with Adam, but

I did not. I took you from him. I created you from a bone that was close to his heart.

So, I shaped the first woman out of a rib, and when the man woke up, I gave her to him to help him. He was supposed to care for you and cherish you. I didn't give him instructions on how to treat you because at the time of creation, he was good. You both were, and sin had not yet been brought into the picture. You came from him, and he was pure. No part of him was evil.

He named you Eve, which means life. He knew you would be the mother of all future human life, and without you, the reproduction of humanity could not take place. Without you, God would have to keep digging in the dirt to create more men. I expected him to treat you the same way he treated himself because, after all, you came from him. I gave you to him to walk with him, help him, love and respect him, and be a companion to him. It was never my intention for you to be stepped on, mistreated, or abused in any way. In fact, none of those things ever took place until sin was introduced into the picture.

The same systems I meticulously created in the garden to cover and care for man were the same systems I designed to cover and care for you. Before the fall in the garden, man didn't have to protect you, man didn't have to provide for you, man didn't have to cover you; I did all of that, but when sin was brought in through rebellion and disobedience, the hierarchy of men over women began as a punishment for sin (Genesis 3:16 NLT & ESV), and that hierarchy has remained in place ever since.

After the garden, the primary role of man was to love, cover, and protect you; to provide for you in every way. But throughout time, instead of man using the strength I gave him to protect, cover, and love you, he has used it instead to steal, cheat, and abuse you; to take from you what he wants without asking you for your love, your heart or your opinion. Not all men have done this, but many have. It was never my intention for there to be a world where men are harming and hurting women. Their women. My women. You were my gift to him, not his doormat.

What Really Happened?

To understand the bigger picture, we must take some time to look at the biblical account of the fall of humanity. It is very important that we review this. We have to discuss what transpired with Eve, the very first woman, but the focus here is certainly not to blame women for everything or in general. Honestly, you've been blamed enough. You've been blamed for wars men decided to fight, blamed for fallen kingdoms ruled by men, blamed, judged, and killed by men for all sorts of reasons and sometimes for no reason at all. You've been blamed for why men abuse you, why men mistreat you, why men don't promote you, why men rape you, and on and on. You've been blamed enough.

There's something that transpired in the garden that we must discuss. Eve, the first woman, found herself one day feeling more comfortable talking to a creature who wasn't at all like her, rather than talking to God or her man. What was it about the serpent that made the woman feel comfortable talking to it? Where was her man? Where was Adam? Was he with her, or was she alone? If he was with her, he was silent, nonresponsive, or emotionally disconnected. It seems Adam was not available, engaged, or around to answer her questions, and she was left to figure things out on her own. What a perfect opportunity for deception to show up.

Why didn't the serpent have a conversation with the man? Why didn't the serpent attempt to talk to Adam? There was something about the woman that drew the serpent to her. Was it her vulnerability, her curiosity, her sensitivity? Or was it her origin? Or maybe it was the first time anyone asked for her opinion, or how she felt about anything?

Perhaps she previously tried to have conversations with Adam, asking him questions about God, about the garden, and about who both of them were. Adam, why am I here? Adam, what are we supposed to be doing? What is a helpmeet? Let's be real! Maybe these are some of the questions Eve asked Adam. Think about the kind of questions and answers that take place in any relationship, especially the relationship of a husband and wife. She might have asked him this: "Can we talk, or is sex and procreation the only thing we are here to do?" Adam, there are questions, needs, concerns, and feelings I have. Adam, I need you. Adam, where are you?

Adam was given the assignment to take care of the garden. Eve was created to be a companion to Adam and to help him. But consider this. Adam never had any say in the matter. While Adam came from the earth, Eve came from him. So perhaps, if the serpent wasn't able to take down Adam directly, he came after what was closest to Adam. He came after his lover, his companion, his helper, his friend, his partner, his wife, and the mother of his children. Yep, that's just like Satan. He chooses those closest to you to tear you down or destroy you, and many times he does this through distance, disagreements, or deception.

According to Webster's dictionary, deception is a strategy designed to make someone believe something that is not true. Satan comes up with a lie he wants you to believe because he knows if you believe that lie and act on it, death, destruction, loneliness, or pain will come to your life. So he works hard to convince you to believe it. That's where deception comes in.

For a lie to work, it has to make sense or come close to making sense. It must be believable and sometimes contains particles of truth.

Deception is a powerful, dangerous strategy utilized to make a lie more believable. Satan is a professional liar and a master deceiver, and once we believe his lies, we sometimes make bad decisions that cause us to feel estranged or disconnected from God. This process leads us down a pathway of believing more and more lies, so much so that we become comfortable living and dwelling in them.

The serpent lied to Eve, and she believed it. Satan is still telling lies to us even today. He continues to lie to us all about who we were created to be. He continues to lie to women about who God created them to be. And, most of all, Satan lies to men about justifying their ungodly treatment of children and women around the world. It's time to tell the truth. It's time to tell you the truth about who you were created to be. It's time to tell the truth about how some have used religion and even the word of God to deceive you and demoralize women even more. It's time to tell you the truth about everything. And, the truth is God loves you more than you could ever dream, comprehend, or imagine, and He wants me to tell you He is truly sorry!

Chapter Two: *Why Me?*

On one hand, I don't know exactly why God chose me, but on the other hand, based on my self-examination and process of elimination, I've come to the following conclusions. First, God needed a man willing to take responsibility for our actions. Yes, Jesus took our sins on the cross, bore our sins, and repaid us with His blood. And within the realm of redemption, there is a role we all must play. Romans 10:9-10 declares, "If you confess with your mouth," meaning he needed a man willing to confess on behalf of men everywhere. I'm willing to be that man.

Secondly, He needed a man who was vulnerable enough to allow God to speak to him in the place of humility and transparency, rather than a defensive, arrogant posture. Many of us men, because of what we have been taught, are not willing to share our feelings. We have convinced boys and men that sharing feelings is a sign of weakness, a sign that we aren't strong or virile. Sharing emotions and feelings is considered by some to be a sign of weakness and something that only women do.

Thirdly, I am acquainted, as many men are, with female familial relationships and female work-related interactions. I have a strong, confident mother and mother-in-law. I've been married for twenty-five plus years to an amazing, intelligent wife who expresses herself confidently and freely. I have three incredible daughters who are very opinionated and outspoken, and I have many other remarkable female friends and relatives. As a husband, father, brother-in-law, and pastor, I've been a part of many conversations that speak to relationships between men and women. And when it comes to sharing feelings, the narrative seems to be the same. Many women share too much, and most men don't share enough, and some don't share at all.

Fourthly, early in life, I was violated by a woman. I've been rejected and hurt by women. And while it produced an element of resentment in me, I wanted to understand what caused the breach between men and women in general. What was it that caused the separation, the breakup, the division that put men and women in positions of superiority and inferiority, rather than working together in a place of harmony?

Next, I consider myself to be a great communicator and a pretty good mediator. I relate well with males and females, extroverts and introverts, the affluent or those in need, and people from different races, cultures, and backgrounds. I usually have good relationships with most people. I've committed my life to doing God's will. I've faithfully and consistently obeyed His voice throughout the years. There are many assignments I have completed for the Kingdom. If I see a need, I usually do something about it. I love to help out wherever and whenever I can.

And finally, I was willing. I don't know if God previously gave this assignment to anyone else who may have declined the offer, but I immediately said yes. Out of everything God has ever asked me to do, this mission to help women understand that they are a top priority on His list is far more important than anything else I have ever done. He wanted me to let women know He loves them and the consistent negativity, the lack of sensitivity, the unholy discourse, the profane and immoral acts directed toward them, and maybe even towards you personally, were never His will or His intention. I gladly accepted the assignment, and here we are.

I also believe God chose me because He has given me the gift of revelation, which is the ability to see spiritual things deeply, and the gift of teaching, which explains the deeper things of the Kingdom, making them easier for others to understand. As a modern-day storyteller, I strive to make the word of God relevant and simpler to comprehend. With the help of the Holy Spirit, I can take complex theology or scripture and make it simple and plain to equip others by helping them understand and apply it to their lives.

At the end of the day, God knows why He has chosen me. He knows I'm usually willing to say yes. I don't know who will stand with me or against me for doing this. I don't know what may come my way because of this book. I don't know if I'll be ostracized or embraced. I do know, to obey is better than sacrifice (1 Samuel 15:22). He assigned me to write this book, to say He was sorry, and to give more clarity about some of the difficulties you might be experiencing in this life's journey. He commissioned me to remind His daughters they are beautiful and wonderfully made (Psalm 139). He called me to be one who would call out the works of darkness and denounce the ungodly treatment of women, especially by men.

He wanted me to make it known that a lot of the chaos, confusion, and contusions we see today in male/female relationships were never His plan. He called me to be a mouthpiece for His daughters to let them know how precious they are to Him. He intends to honor them, not just in heaven but right here on earth. He has called me to encourage you and uplift you from the bonds and chains of the enemy. Here I am. I have said, "Yes."

Chapter Three: *What Happened At Twelve?*

I think it's important to know how much sin has perverted the natural course of life God genuinely blessed us with. It's insidious, diabolical, and wicked. Every creature on the planet, all created by God, has a natural course of maturity. Nothing stays the same. Just like there are seasons of the weather, there are seasons in the lives of males and females. We start out as infants, cooing and crawling, trying to understand and experience our surroundings through all of our senses. We grab, touch, taste, feel, hear, and see. We respond to voices and smells. As we grow and mature, we walk, talk, and mimic the world around us.

As young children, we are explorers. And we soon discover we are not alone. We are surrounded by people who look like us, sound like us, and are intricately involved in our growth and development. We can tell who Mama is and who Daddy is. We become familiar with the sights, sounds, and smells of our environment. We come in contact with other humans. And when we are young, we see each other the same. The fact that we are different does not exist. Boys and girls play together. We are one. We are friends.

We play video games together and look at bugs and stars at the same time. We take turns on swings at playgrounds and watch cartoons, giggling about the characters and their funny shapes and sounds. We beg for other kids' meals, sharing fries and cookies. We are the same. The world is one big amusement park, and we are all laughing and screaming on the same ride. Initially, the dreams we had to be an astronaut, a president, a CEO, an entertainer, or an athlete were at the forefront. We realize our amazing potential to be anything we want. We even have answers to solve world hunger and world peace. We are superheroes with superpowers. We see ourselves as the literal "savior" of our families, our siblings, our communities, and our world.

But something interesting started to happen. Things began to change. God revealed to me that little girls in America die around the age of 12. It's not a physical death, but a mental, emotional, and psychological demise. Many girls lose the joy of being a child. At that age, there is the transition from the innocence and similarity of childhood to the hierarchy of the sexes. Now we go from a fun, innocent, level playing field to who's the prettiest, who's the most popular, what group should I associate with, and how to transition from out to in. It's in this transition from elementary school to middle school, from preschool to preteen, where puberty diminishes purity and equality gives way to difference and deviation. Around the age of twelve, sexual perversions can become prevalent. Molestation and sexual abuse are usually more common around the age of twelve. Now, a distorted view of self, as well as the world around us, emerges. But this doesn't have to be a permanent state.

What is natural in God's plan will become perverted if not managed appropriately. Now we've gone from the playground that united us to the mental, emotional amusement park of physical attraction and sexual magnetism. In middle school, at twelve, the focus changes from just having fun and being a kid to being conformed to the image of others or being pressured to represent something that projects sexuality, sensuality, and perceived adult conduct. Behaviors become different, while clothes and hairstyles change. Family interactions, domestic relationships, and personal encounters now determine the trajectory of "turning twelve." And, without the godly maturity necessary to direct, instruct, and facilitate this metamorphosis, perversion is inevitable.

At twelve, our bodies are experiencing emotions we are unfamiliar with. Sensations, feelings, and physical consciousness take place. Our conversations shift from cartoon characters to expressions of ideas and beliefs acquired from our environment. Healthy rites of passage are often limited depending on the socio-economic status and cultural influence. And, just like Eve in the Garden, we are subject to the manipulation, persuasion, and bias of ungodly thoughts, actions, attitudes, and ideas.

At twelve, we're desperate for information. What's happening to us? How are we supposed to act? What are we supposed to do? Who am I? Where do I fit in? It's a new season of questions. Imagine five cars coming down five different streets at a high speed with no traffic lights, all colliding with each other at the same time. Instead of having debates about who was the fastest or who could throw the ball the farthest, the conversation is now around lips, hips, and fingertips. If you're a girl, what does that mean? If you're a boy, what does that mean? How are we supposed to act or behave, especially since our bodies are changing? These are the questions of the soul, the mind, the will, and the emotions. And the answers received will determine the type of adult we become.

Turning twelve often means that our identity is no longer immersed in our ability to skip a rock or catch a lightning bug. Here, our identity is now attached to our senses and our physical makeup. Whether it's our height, shoe size, breasts, or hip size, we become obsessed with physical appearance rather than emotional intelligence, spiritual maturity, and community awareness. And, sometimes, no one is there to guide us, or the examples we see point us the wrong way.

For some now, success as a twelve-year-old is determined by how many followers you have on social media, what type of electronic devices you have, what your body looks like, how many sexual encounters you have had, how many designer items are in your closet, and whether you qualify to be somebody's significant other.

Success is measured by reality shows where the focus is on who is in love with whom, who is the best at manipulating people, and any other social media influence observed. At twelve, our focus now determines our outcomes. And, if not redirected, we begin to engage in destructive thought processes that have us seeing success as being how many boyfriends, girlfriends, cars, sneakers, or followers we have.

The most powerful tool we were given by God is our imagination. At twelve, our imaginations are working overtime, moving beyond time and space. We see the potential in everything. Whether under negative or positive influence, twelve is where we are creative problem solvers and innovative thinkers. Our cognitive ability, our intellect, and our ability to recognize and comprehend complex ideas surface, yet at the same time our physical bodies are moving at light speed, and the collision of understanding and wisdom, for our bodies and our minds, has not taken place.

This is the perfect environment for Satan to do his best to distort our thinking, our responses, and our emotions in an effort to derail the plan of God for us as adults one day. Whether he does it through a relative, a video, a friend's secret, or the images we are constantly bombarded with, twelve is a critical number. It is the difference between Jairus' daughter asleep and Jesus in the temple teaching. That moment determines what it all can potentially look like. But just remember, Jairus' daughter got up, and Jesus went on to become the Savior of the world. And so can you. You can arise too.

Chapter Four: *The Truth of the Matter*

Satan doesn't want you to know what's really going on. Why does abandonment, rejection, low self-esteem, and depression enter into the lives of women early? Why does the enemy want us to feel incompetent prematurely? Why does Satan want our emotions out of control quickly? Why does Satan want you to feel as though you're not able to be the person you initially came into the world to be? Satan's goal is to steal, kill, and destroy (John 10:10). He wants to steal the creativity and imagination of our youth. He wants to kill the dreams we dreamt of when our young minds were vivid and innocent. He wants to destroy our generations by planting seeds of shame, guilt, bitterness, perversion, and hostility so we can plant those same seeds in the lives of our children, our environment, our community, and our world.

Did you realize while God has a plan for us, so does Satan? You're probably saying, "Pastor Das, of course I knew that." You've said it before. Satan's plan is to steal, kill, and destroy. Yes, I did. Yet, I never said when. What would happen if you considered all you went through, as a little girl, a teenager, a young woman, and perhaps even now, was and is part of a hellish scheme to keep you, not only from your destiny, not only from your future, not only from your blessings, but simply from a relationship? Yes, a relationship. It's the kind of relationship that affirms who you are and confirms what you're capable of. Isn't that interesting? Most, if not all, of our negative encounters as children are centered around relationships. It's the one thing we learn early to either cherish or hate. And when that is damaged, when a relationship is broken, restoration is often difficult.

So how can we see ourselves fearfully and wonderfully made (Psalm 139) when we're always fearful and constantly wondering? How can one be great when we no longer see hope in ourselves or others? How can we consider the unlimited possibilities and endless opportunities God has designed and created for us when all we encounter is consistent negativity, never-ending abuse, and continuous pain? The truth of the matter is, Satan doesn't want us to know the truth, the real truth about who we really are, how powerful we are, and how resilient and beautiful God made us to be.

Satan's goal is for us to be "estranged" from God. His desire is for us to be out of touch with God, so we are never in touch with who God had in mind for us to be. Any way he can put a wedge between our God nature and God our creator is his ultimate goal. For if we never activate our God nature, then we can never become fully aware of who God intended for us to be. We were created in the image and likeness of the Triune God. We were designed to have the power of the Father, the dominion of Jesus Christ the Son, and the authority of the Holy Spirit. And, with that power, authority, and dominion, we have the mandate to be fruitful, multiply, and replenish. Jesus told Peter in Luke 22:31, "Satan wants to sift you like wheat." In other words, we would become so dehumanized and demoralized that anything God says to us, about us, we wouldn't believe.

The free online dictionary defines the word 'estranged' as a loss of affection, a loss of a former closeness, and a turning away from someone. Being estranged means a loss of connection. It's like being blocked from a friend's Facebook or Instagram page. It's like being removed from a group chat or online game team. It's like walking into a crowded room and feeling all alone. It's like suddenly feeling like you're no longer a part of someone's world, someone you may have known for years; someone who was very close, and now all of a sudden you've been 'unfriended'! Satan wants you to unfriend God or feel "unfriended" by Him. In essence, Satan wants you and God to become estranged.

As a child, I remember my parents would disagree, but ultimately, they always came back together. While they had their differences, they found a way to navigate through those differences and come back to a place of the re-establishment of their covenant. But what happens when there are no reconciliations and no restoration of relationships? What happens when we are "estranged" from family, friends, or community? What happens when Satan succeeds and we are estranged from God?

If a thief comes into your house and takes items out of your attic, your basement, or your storage containers, you probably won't notice it right away. While those items are part of our lives, your immediate relationship with them is distant, detached, and remote. But when a thief comes into your space and takes items you use often or have a close relationship with, you will notice.

Now what happens when estrangement takes place early? What happens when we lose something or someone before we even realize our need for them? Satan is an expert in estrangement. He comes for our relationship with God prior to the revelation of who God is in our lives. He comes for our relationships with fathers and mothers prior to the revelation of their importance in our lives.

Addiction, rejection, depression, abandonment, and the like are all forms of estrangement. Addiction estranges us from children in the womb, a family who loves us, and a community wanting to support us. Rejection estranges us from the sacred fellowship of one another. We begin to see each other as literal enemies and decline to enter into covenant relationships because we are afraid of being betrayed. Depression estranges us from our own mind, body, and spirit. We are unable to embrace the joy of our existence and the abundant life we were created to experience. Abandonment estranges us from the very ones assigned to protect us, care for us, encourage, and facilitate our development. And Satan is laughing the whole time.

Jairus' daughter was estranged. She was estranged from the life she had been given. She was estranged from the dreams and vivid imagination of a child, a young girl. She was estranged from her relationship with her mother and father. She was estranged from a beloved community that mourned her death and counted her out.

The woman with the issue of blood lived twelve years of her life in an estranged state. Not only was she losing her life, but as a woman, she was losing the lives of those she was destined to carry (Mark 5:25-34). While men live in a constant state of virility, women carry a covenant of life in their womb; lives in the form of ova that are only available to them for a certain period of time. And the truth of the matter is Satan enjoys our estrangement, so he uses this tactic all the time. Estrangement compels us to devalue one another, denigrate each other, abuse, defame, and malign each other. Being estranged means not understanding we were both designed to mirror the image of God, and to see that same image in one another.

And yet, estrangement is not always external; sometimes, the deepest separation happens within us. Hadassah carried this kind of estrangement—one not just from others, but from herself.

And that's the truth of the matter.

Chapter Five: *Who Is Esther?*

Esther knew a lot about estrangement. She was an Israelite, a Hebrew child, and a member of the chosen people who were rebellious and defiant. Due to their disobedience and idolatry, God permitted them to experience Babylonian captivity for a period of seventy years. And now, as a child, originally named Hadassah, she's a part of this estrangement. She has lost connection with her family, her environment, and her previous life. Here she is, now growing up an orphan, taken in by a family member, her uncle Mordecai.

It was the custom of the Hebrew culture that if a child was orphaned, they were immediately raised by their extended family. A male relative was required, by law, to take them in. How many of us have found ourselves in situations we did not create? Raised by grandparents, aunts and uncles, family members, or close friends, through no fault of our own. Circumstances and situations, beyond our control, placed us in positions where we literally had no input over our immediate present situation. And, depending on whose care we were in, determined what, or who, we would encounter in our young, impressionable lives.

Hadassah means 'myrtle tree,' a tree associated with prosperity, peace, and love. What peace would she find? What love would she have? What prosperity was in her future? Hadassah had no idea. She not only found herself in a foreign house but also a foreign country. She didn't ask for this. Her hopes and dreams were now at the mercy of someone else. Her vision of who she was and who she would become was now null and void. And she had no say in how her own life would evolve.

Estrangement is a funny thing. It's transferable. It has a ripple effect. Here she is estranged from her home, not because of her actions, but the actions of the adults around her. She wasn't responsible for their inability to follow God's words. She wasn't accountable for their unwillingness to worship the God of Abraham, Isaac, and Jacob. She didn't cause this problem. And, yet, what has happened to her is the direct result of someone else's actions. Remember in Chapter 3, we stated that Satan comes for our relationship with God prior to the revelation of who God is in our lives. She is now put in a position where estrangement is the order of the day. Her name has to change.

Esther was invented, created, and manufactured to survive the space in which Hadassah found herself. Her lifestyle is different. She has gone from an agricultural background to being one in a harem of women groomed and designated to be the sexual partner of a foreign king. Who she was now is no longer relevant, important, or significant. She has now been renamed, retitled, and realigned because of someone else's actions. Her heritage, who she was created to be, and her Jewish history, appeared to no longer carry any weight. What she didn't realize was that Esther means Persian star, and she was about to have a starring role, not in her own plan, but in the amazing plan of God.

Chapter Six: *Esther's Dilemma*

Now, having been raised in Mordecai's house, her entrance into this new place is to be initiated into the king's harem. Babylonian culture dictated the king had access to the young men and young women of those who were conquered. Their appearance, beauty, good looks, and intelligence further made them candidates for the king's court. It was Hananiah (Shadrach), Azariah (Meshach), and Michial's (Abendego's) intelligence and good looks that gave them access to the king's court. It was Daniel's (Belteshazzar's) wisdom and ability to interpret dreams that made him a governor in the Babylonian political structure. After years of preparation and months of training, Esther finds herself in the king's court, favored by the king.

It appears Mordecai has raised Hadassah in such a way that she makes an impression on the king and the caretaker of the king's harem. And Esther is positioned in the forefront. What was it that made her unique? What was it that made her different? Her uncle Mordecai raised her according to Jewish laws and traditions. While the Bible doesn't speak to Mordecai's household dynamics, Hadassah's ability to evolve into Esther speaks volumes. But an unexpected situation occurs.

There is a moment where not only is Hadassah threatened, but her whole lineage, including her uncle Mordecai, is at risk. A sly member of the king's court, Haman, has an issue with Mordecai that ultimately leads to the decree demanding death for all the Jews. And Esther is the answer. Mordecai calls on her to remember that she is Hadassah, and using her resources and access, Esther has to persuade the king to overturn the decree, therefore saving all of their lives, including her own.

What do I do now? Hadassah represents the pain of her past. Hadassah represents the sum total of her inability to be in control of the trajectory of her life. Hadassah represented a lower, weaker version of herself. To her, nothing good could have come out of being Hadassah. Like many of us, who have sequestered our Hadassahs, embraced our Esthers, and moved on, no matter how hard we try, we cannot fully escape who Hadassah is, what she encountered, and what she has been through. We cannot run away from the devastating events of our childhood. We are unable to break away from the Hadassah, who was labeled stupid, ugly, dumb, and pitiful. Hadassah is the child who may have been raped, molested, abused, and misused. Hadassah is the little girl who was criticized, marginalized, and diminished. Hadassah is the teenager who had the baby, had the abortion, made the mistake, and ran away from it all.

Has it ever occurred to you that they both have value? It's easier to see the value in Esther because her value shines through. Her value can be seen on the outside. Her value is wrapped in fame and fortune. She is popular, prosperous, and powerful. She is seen, heard, and well-known, and her bank account isn't too shabby either. Everyone wants to be like Esther or have an 'Esther' as a friend or partner. Esther has knowledge. Esther has resources. Esther has connections in high places. But our Hadassah is as valuable as our Esther is. Together they are the sum total of all God intended for us to be. In Psalm 139, David writes, "All the days of my life were written in your book before you even knew me." God created Hadassah, and God empowered Esther. No, they are not a split personality; they both are the result of the complex creativity of God. Hadassah has wisdom and strength from what she has been through. Esther has the favor, knowledge, and resources to move things forward. They both have a purpose, and they both can be used by God.

Chapter Seven: *What Happened to Hadassah?*

At some point, God will ask the question, "Where is Hadassah? What did you do with her? Did we leave Hadassah behind? When did we execute the process of withholding Hadassah so we could become Esther instead? When did we choose to disown Hadassah because Esther has everything we ever wanted or ever dreamed we could have? Esther represents the sum total of everything we were able to accomplish in spite of Hadassah and because of Hadassah, all at the same time.

In spite of Hadassah, we were able to finish school. Because of Hadassah, we had the strength to stay in class. In spite of Hadassah, we have access to rooms and tables Esther can go into and sit. Because of Hadassah, we found ourselves knowing how to plan, strategize, and survive in the environment where Esther dwells. In spite of Hadassah, we have degrees and positions enabling us to operate in circles of influence beyond our imagination. Because of Hadassah, we were able to use our influence to help others less fortunate than ourselves. In spite of Hadassah, we have the ability to stand before influencers and wealthy experts. Because of Hadassah, when the storms of life come, we are able to stand and endure.

And yet no one ever sees Hadassah. It appears no one experiences our Hadassah or even knows that she ever existed. We have covered her up, buried her, and muted her voice. It appears that Hadassah has died. Has it ever occurred to us that God needs both? At some point, we all have to choose to resurrect Hadassah or just let her die. God needs our Hadassah to remember so that our Esther has a reason to stand up and fight. Hadassah is the fuel, and Esther is the fire.

Have you ever played a card game? When you play cards, you usually have to work with the hand you're dealt. And often, the cards you get can determine the outcome of your game. Where you were born, how you were raised, where you lived, went to school, your ethnicity or race, your socio-economic status, and so on. These are the cards we were dealt. They are the things in our origin that we cannot go back and change. These are the attributes we cannot wish away. They are who we are, no matter where we are. And yet, even while she was Esther, there came a moment when Hadassah and her experiences, her heritage, her lineage, and her belief system were necessary for Esther herself to live. And while Hadassah may not have necessarily liked her initial circumstances, Esther needed both of them for her to live as well.

Hadassah was an orphan; Esther was a queen. Hadassah was a young girl with no rights; Esther was a powerful woman with the favor of the King. Hadassah had no voice; Esther could speak loudly and was easily heard. Hadassah was Mordecai's adopted daughter; Esther was the preference of the king. Hadassah perhaps saw herself as a victim, but Esther was victorious; she was an overcomer. Hadassah wore hand-me-downs. Esther wears the latest in designer clothes. Hadassah was isolated and alone. Esther had people who adored her. Hadassah was abused; Esther has control. Hadassah the teenager had the baby; Esther is the perfect wife and mom.

Hadassah had dreams; Esther makes dreams come true. Hadassah had no power; Esther is very powerful. But neither one is separate from the other. They both are the same person.

Both are needed, both are important, and both are critical in order to live fully. God created Hadassah. She carries the birthright and the anointing, but Esther has access and authority. Esther is the alabaster box, but Hadassah is the oil concealed within. Where is your Hadassah? What have you done with her? Have you buried her so as to forget what you have been through? Did you bury her along with the trauma of your childhood? Is she lying in the grave of a past or present abusive relationship? Is she interred in the poverty of childhood? Is Hadassah in the cemetery of your addiction, alcoholism, or your years of being bullied and abused? No matter where she is, Esther had to face her. Esther needed her for them to accomplish their true purpose, the saving of their nation; the saving of their people.

You see, while Esther spoke to the king, it was Hadassah who called the people to fast and pray. While it was Esther who confronted Haman, the enemy of the Jews, it was Hadassah who produced a strategy to defeat him. While it was Esther who risked her life to enter the king's court, it was really Hadassah who said, "If I perish, let me perish.". Finally, for Hadassah and Esther, saving her people became more important than saving her own life.

Let me be clear here. I never said this would be easy. I know it seems easier to say, "I'm okay." I know it seems less stressful to stay right where you are right now. But the pain, the shame, the hurt won't go away. It will remain within until one day, that pain, that shame will show up, usually at the most inconvenient moment. It will show up when you least expect it, and your control over it will be limited. There is a point in our lives when our healing must be more important than shame, embarrassment, or what others may think. Esther could not be Esther without Hadassah, and Hadassah was who Esther needed. In the end, God uses both.

Chapter Eight: *Resurrecting Hadassah*

I've come to realize a scab over a wound does not mean it's healed. And, while scabs are designed to protect wounds and stop infection, the damaged area must have been thoroughly cleaned previously, and the scab must be given adequate time to harden so the work beneath it can be accomplished successfully. An improperly formed scab can give us a false sense of hope or healing. We see the scab and automatically think all is well underneath. But if something or someone pokes, touches, or bumps into the wound, we're immediately reminded that the sore is still there. Digging up the past and resurrecting Hadassah is not always an easy task.

How many times are we reminded that Hadassah is still there? Is it the moment you walk into the room and encounter your abusive ex? Is it when you see a mother pushing a stroller talking to a cooing baby and the pain of your abortion rises up? Does it happen when you notice a child being yelled at in a grocery store and you are reminded of the ugly words spoken to you when you were small? Or when you attend the family reunion, and the relative who molested and raped you shows up?

Scripture tells us that when Joseph saw his brothers, even though they did not recognize him, he wept (Gen. 43:30). These were the ones who conspired to kill him, sold him into slavery, and then lied to his father about his presumed death. He was second in command in Egypt, but his Hadassah remembered. David, the shepherd boy who was anointed king and a minstrel to Saul, mistreated by his father and his brothers, wrote in Psalm 23:5, "You prepare a table before me in the presence of my enemies; You anoint my head with oil; My cup runs over." Even in the midst of an overflowing cup, his Hadassah remembered.

Naomi, once full of life, love, and wealth, returns to her homeland broken, destitute, and ashamed. Her name means 'pleasant.' Yet when greeted by her kinsmen and women, she declares in Ruth 1:20-21, "Do not call me Naomi; call me Mara, for the Almighty has dealt very bitterly with me. I went out full, and the Lord has brought me home again empty." Her Hadassah, remembered. The woman with the issue of blood, confused and lifeless, touched the hem of Jesus's garment (Luke 8:43-48). When she was healed, and Jesus inquired, "Who touched me?" she didn't answer. Now healed, able to walk away from a place she had to crawl to, she was initially afraid to answer because her Hadassah was remembered as well.

And now Esther is in a position where the only one who has the answer to her dilemma is the Hadassah she has tried to forget. A nation of Jewish people is on the brink of extinction, and while Esther has the connection, Hadassah has the strategy. Esther has the face, but Hadassah has the strength. Esther is the queen, but Hadassah is the warrior. Esther has the access, but Hadassah has the anointing.

What will you do when our Father in heaven has need for your Hadassah but you have chosen to live only as Esther? Esther has to make the choice. Esther has to make the decision. Esther has the power and authority to raise Hadassah or leave her to die. How important is Hadassah to Esther's story? She was very important. How important is your Hadassah to your Esther story? Only God knows, but it's up to you to decide. You have the choice to decide whether your Hadassah lives or dies. God has the power to do it, but you have the choice to decide. For many, resurrecting Hadassah is like removing a scab covering, a still active wound. Are you willing to peel it back? Are you willing to resurrect your Hadassah so that both she and Esther will be saved? I wish to encourage you to do so.

Satan's job is to stop us from addressing the scab or the wound. His goal is to keep you from peeling back the layers of hurt, pain, shame, and guilt so that your past cannot be dealt with and you might never fully heal. He's good with you remaining as Esther all of your life. He's great when Esther is the only one you're willing to love, relate to, and keep in the forefront. Esther the beautiful. Esther the favored. Esther the intelligent. Esther the wonderful. Esther the sophisticated. Esther the popular. Esther the queen.

But what do you do when certain circumstances require Hadassah to show up? What do you do when God has need for Hadassah? Hadassah the molested. Hadassah the raped. Hadassah the abused. Hadassah the isolated. Hadassah the stupid. Hadassah the disgraced. Hadassah the shamed. Hadassah the orphaned. Isn't it amazing how God can use the worst moments in our lives to produce the best in us? Your Esther is not just a product of your Hadassah experience. Your Esther can be even greater with your Hadassah resurrected. It was Esther that called for prayer and fasting, but it was Hadassah that knew prayer and fasting were necessary. Why? Because while she was Hadassah, and she had nothing else, or no one else, prayer and fasting and crying out to God was what kept her from losing her mind.

Jesus went into the grave. His body was beaten, disfigured, and damaged beyond recognition. But in a resurrected state, he does not look like the Hadassah experience he had been through. For three days, Jesus stayed in His Hadassah experience, seemingly hopeless. The tomb was closed. The scab covered the wound. He was literally in the grave. He literally went to "hell." It was the hell others were in. It was the hell others had been through. There are some alive today, but their situations are so bad that it feels like they're currently living in hell.

For some, perhaps hell & Hadassah were or even now are still one and the same. But, Jesus encountered the pain of those trapped in their Hadassah experience. During his death, Jesus literally stepped into hell and took the keys of death and hell from the enemy. He used his Hadassah experience to win the victory! Revisiting your Hadassah experience is where you will get your keys, your healing, your victory.

I know this might be difficult. Revisiting trauma usually is. I'm certainly not asking you to exhume all of your Hadassah experiences immediately. What I am suggesting is that unless the past pain of Hadassah is fully healed, Esther cannot fully be all she has been called to be, nor fully do all that she has been called to do. I realize some of our past experiences may have been painful, traumatic, and disturbing, to say the least, but sometimes being in touch with who we were is vital for our discovery of who we are truly supposed to be.

Chapter Nine: *Daughter Arise*

Here was the little girl, once full of life and laughter, now lying still, her small body a stark reminder of the fragility of life. Her body now represented all she had been through. Her dreams had died. Her voice was gone. Her energy dissipated. Perhaps her eyes were cloudy and the bright light that once shined in them was gone. It would appear like there was no need for anyone to attempt to do anything, including her.

But then... Jesus arrives. His presence brings a shift in the atmosphere. He looked at the mourners and said, "Why all this commotion and wailing? The child is not dead. She is only sleeping." Clear the room! Clear the room! It's too crowded! Clear the room! There are too many people in the room. Too many negative thoughts are in the room. Too much doubt is in the room. Too much skepticism is in the room. Too much criticism is in the room. The hater is in the room. The liar is in the room. The violator is in the room. The murderer is in the room. There's too much junk in the room.

Jesus's first act, when stepping into Jairus' house, was to clear his daughter's room of what was unnecessary. He cleared the room of unnecessary people, unnecessary thoughts, and unnecessary judgments. He cleared the room of anything that would interfere with the awakening of the girl. Why? So, the only thing she would focus on was Him. For He was the only one who could wake her up.

At that moment, a convergence happened. The spirit of the little girl had to make a choice. Would she succumb to the voices of those who declared she was dead? Or would she respond to the one who made her? The one who loved her. The one who knew her before she was even born. The one who knew her more than anyone else could ever know her. The one who has a perfect plan for her life. The one who knew it wasn't over for her, but the best was yet to come. How would she respond? Would she even be willing? Did she see herself as important enough, loved enough, and meaningful enough to respond to His voice?

In Esther's story, Esther had to call on Hadassah and bring her back to life. The Hadassah who was considered dead would have to somehow come alive so that she and Esther, together, could walk into their destiny. When Jesus walked into that room, He saw this situation entirely different than anyone else's capacity to understand. While others saw the little girl as dead, unresponsive, incapable of movement, and unable to function as living and breathing, Jesus merely saw her as "sleeping."

Undeterred, Jesus approaches where the little girl lay, on her bed of pain and suffering, on her bed of memories of bodily harm and the names she was called. On her bed of violation and powerlessness. On her bed of failures, faults, and false narratives. On her bed of distrust, denial, deception, and disappointment. Jesus clears the room and does something remarkable. He speaks words that will echo throughout this little girl's mind for the rest of her life. Taking her by the hand, Jesus declares, "Talitha, cumi," which means, "Little girl, I say to you, Arise!" (Mark 5:41).

In that moment, life came back. Not a partial life, but a full life. Not a life that denied her experiences, but one that fully embraced her past state, her present condition, and, most importantly, her amazing future. She was alive, not just in body, but also in spirit. The little girl who had been lost was found, resurrected from her dead state, and she emerged hungry and ready for more life. Jesus instructs them to give her something to eat. It is a moment when this little girl realizes she is not just hungry for food but hungry for life. A full life. A better life. A new life. The past, with all its pain and sorrow, would forever be a part of her story, but it could no longer limit her present or hinder her spectacular future.

It was a new beginning. A beginning that embraced everything about her. Who she was, who she is, and who she was going to be. Nothing needed to be hidden anymore; nothing had to be underground, masked, covert, or secret any longer. When people encountered her, they would not only know who she had been, the once-dead little girl, but they would also know that she is alive, resurrected, and ready to embrace all of who she was and would be; like Esther's resurrection of Hadassah, now in sync with one another, appreciating the past that would be her launching into her future.

In the days that followed, she would come to understand the depth of her resurrection. She would learn to integrate the dichotomy of her experiences, to acknowledge the wounds of her past while embracing the promise of her future. She would grow into a woman of strength and grace, her life a testament to the power of Jesus' love and the resilience of the human spirit.

And so, the little girl who had once been lost was found. She arose, not just from her bed, but from the ashes of her past. She stood tall, her heart filled with hope and determination. She was no longer defined by her pain, but by her resurrection. She was alive, and she was hungry for more.

So, I say to you, you who have had the courage to read these pages to the end: all of your story matters. And yes, while God is sorry for all you have experienced, for what was taken away from you, marred and distorted, mishandled, misaligned, and mismanaged, none of it can interfere with His plan to use all of it, to use all of you, for His glory! Yet nothing can compare to what God has for you now. Nothing can compare to how God will use everything, your 'perceived' death, your so-called demise, that moment where you felt you lost it all; it cannot compare to the glorious plan He has for you.

Just as Jairus had to allow Jesus into the room of his daughter, you'll have to allow Jesus into the room of your heart. And when He comes in, you have to allow Him into the room of your pain, the room of your hurt, your guilt, and your shame. When you let Him into the room, what you once perceived as a place of death now has become a habitation of an abundant new life.

Think about how those individuals who resigned you to death, those who mocked, ridiculed, teased you, and laughed at the prospect of your return, are now having to watch your rise to success, your ability to get up and keep going, your capacity to run, even when you were broken, discouraged, and damaged. Here you are, ready to embrace all of who you are, the fullness of life, the completeness of who you are as a newly resurrected person, your Hadassah, your Esther, heart to heart, hand in hand. The woman you are now and the little girl, resurrected, restored, and realigned together for a fabulous future. We say to you, "Daughter, arise!"

Conclusion

Daughter Arise is more than a book. It is a brand-new community specially designed for women. It is a glorious movement of women helping each other to arise. In the fall of 2021, we held our first international online women's event, and we have continued to have several events since then. The theme verse for The Daughter Arise Movement is Mark 5:41, which says, "Taking her by the hand, Jesus said to her, "*Talitha, cumi*," which means, "Little girl, I say to you, arise!""

The term 'Arise,' in our context, means:

1. Identifying barriers that prevent women from moving beyond their negative life experiences

2. Gracefully and successfully moving those barriers out of the way

3. Connecting women to a healthy community where they can be helped, healed, and inspired.

There are many barriers that threaten to hold women down. Whether external or internal, these boundaries can cause feelings of guilt, shame, frustration, abandonment, isolation, depression, and defeat.

Our goal is to encourage and uplift women with our positive community filled with women who have overcome difficulties and obstacles themselves, while at the same time helping women to become keenly aware of their already God-given abilities to overcome it all.

What if I told you Daughter Arise offers the opportunity for you to move beyond your barriers, beyond your limitations, and beyond your self-imposed restrictions? What if I declared to you that your ability to arise will take place and cannot be hindered by any barricade, blockade, or blockage? We want you to arise from sickness, pain, sorrow, suffering, shame, and any mental or emotional death. We want you to emerge from loneliness, insecurity, codependency, bad habits, addictions, and the power of all negative influences. We want you to come out of guilt, fear, low self-esteem, abandonment, rejection, and depression. We say to you, "Daughter, arise!" (Please visit us online at DaughterArise.org.)

Reflections

Please take the time to pray and reflect after reading this book. Get a notebook, a journal, or a few sheets of paper and get ready to write. We hope what you have read brings clarity and healing, and that you are being prepared for the road ahead.

Chapter One – I'm Sorry

1. How are you doing with accepting the apology?

2. Is there anyone or more than one person who you wish would apologize to you and say sorry? If they were to apologize, what would you want them to say?

3. Is there anyone that you need to apologize to? You might not be able to do it at this time, but if you could, what would you say to them?

Chapter Two – Why Me?

This particular chapter is very personal to me, and I had to be very vulnerable in order to write it.

1. How do you think it was written?

2. Do you think it brought forth a positive and helpful message?

3. What do you think I should have said differently in this chapter? (I would sincerely love to hear from you on this).

Chapter Three – What Happened at Twelve?

1. Write a little bit about what your life was like when you were 12.

2. Do you remember anything? Did you have any happy memories? Any sad ones?

3. Who were the people who were in your life at that time?

4. Was there anyone that you were particularly fond of?

5. Was there anyone that you were particularly afraid of?

6. Who made the greatest impression on you at that time?

7. Do you remember your favorite song?

8. Who was your best friend? What did you wish and hope for?

9. Who did you want to become?

10. What kind of questions did you have back then?

11. If you could go back in time and tell the younger you anything, what would it be and why? Think about it and write it down.

Chapter Four – The Truth of the Matter

1. Take some time to describe yourself. I mean, really describe yourself.

2. What do you think about yourself? Feel free to be as truthful as you can with the understanding that we all have

things about our lives that we would like to improve or change.

3. Please list the things that you like about yourself because it's important to acknowledge those things as well. Some things that you do well and that you are known for. Hopefully, those things are positive and productive. If they are not, still list them, but consider making changes where needed so that you can better yourself.

4. Have you ever been estranged from someone? Please take the time to write it out. This exercise may help you to deal with it better.

5. Take some time to describe your relationship with God. Do you believe in him? If you do, do you feel close to him? If you don't, in what ways would you like to see your relationship with Him become better?

6. What are some things you feel have been stolen from you over the years? Of course these can actually be objects, but I'm more talking about things within your heart, your thoughts, your emotions, your self-esteem, things like that. Name some people, relationships, experiences, objects, or opportunities that you lost along the way and that you wish you could have back.

7. What are some habits, behaviors, or ways of thinking, or even people, that you wish you could get rid of?

Chapter Five—Who Is Esther?

1. Have you ever been fake or phony? Let's talk about it.

2. Have you ever put on a fake front or presented yourself to be something or someone that you are not just so you can fit in? Maybe there are some areas where you're still doing that now? Sometimes you do this for survival. Sometimes you do this because it's a part of our profession or our job. Sometimes we do this because we have children watching us. Sometimes we do this because we are fearful for our lives. Sometimes you do this because we have lost touch with who we really are, and we have become somewhat that we are now more familiar with. That's easier. Just to keep doing what we're doing right now. You have to take the time to go back and discover who we were or who we are supposed to be.

3. What's the one decision you wish you could go back and change or take back? Can you think of a time when you wish you had been genuine and sincere about your thoughts and feelings instead of saying something just to please others or just saying what you wanted others to hear, or just saying what you thought you were supposed to say instead of what you wanted to say? In your own words, tell me what you think.

4. Hadassah took the journey of becoming Esther and then living that and being comfortable with that. Do you think it was easy? Do you think it was hard? Why or why not? What would you have done if you were in Esther or Hades's shoes?

Chapter Six – Esther's Dilemma

Have you ever been in a situation where you did not want to revisit the past? Maybe you wish that something had never happened to you, but it did. Maybe you wish that family members and others would never talk about it again, but sometimes they do. Maybe you wish you could go back and change the past, but you can't.

Maybe healing will take place if you at least revisit some of those areas of hurt and pain with the right help. The right support. The right people or person who can walk you through the corridors of your past, revisiting the pain while receiving counsel on restoration and healing.

In Esther's case, she could not move forward unless she first went back. No, we shouldn't backslide, nor should we look back like Lot's wife did, but sometimes we do need to go back because there are clues about our future, clues about our destiny, clues about areas in our lives that need to be addressed and dealt with correctly.

We don't always have to go back, but sometimes we do. Make sure you are ready for it. Maybe you have done some things in your past. God already tells us that in Christ Jesus, there is no condemnation—only love, acceptance, forgiveness, and healing. But we cannot do it alone; we need His help. We must lean on, trust, and rely on God for everything.

1. What past experiences or wounds have you been avoiding, and how might revisiting them with the right support bring healing and clarity to your journey?

2. Like Esther, are there areas in your life where you need to look back in order to move forward? What lessons, patterns, or insights from your past might be shaping your future?

3. How can you fully embrace God's love, acceptance, forgiveness, and healing in your life? What steps can you take to lean on, trust, and rely on Him more deeply?

Chapter Seven – What Happened to Hadassah?

This is a deep chapter. This is a deep question. What happened to Hadassah?

1. What happened to you? Please write whatever you feel about this. Writing it out may bring healing to you.

2. Also, this could be a great place to talk about times in your life when you felt left out, unrecognized, made fun of,

belittled, ignored, or left behind. Maybe someone literally betrayed you. This is the time to think about and write about all of that.

Chapter Eight—Resurrecting Hadassah (Hadassah Lives Again)

I know this might be difficult—revisiting trauma usually is. I'm not asking you to exhume all of your Hadassah experiences at once. What I am suggesting is this: unless the past wounds of Hadassah are fully healed, Esther cannot fully become all she is meant to be, nor can she step fully into her calling. Some of our past experiences have been painful, even traumatic. But sometimes, reconnecting with who we were is essential for discovering who we are truly meant to be.

1. What are some of the things you wanted to do when you were a little girl?

2. What did you dream of?

3. What did you want to become?

4. Did you feel close to God as a young child?

God wants to give you freedom right now. No matter what's going on around you, just like when there was a storm, Jesus was asleep in the boat because He knew how to have peace in the midst of the storm. God wants the same for you.

Chapter Nine – Daughter Arise

As we come to the end of this journey together, I want to take a moment to reflect on the heart of Daughter Arise. This book was born out of a deep desire to empower women, to inspire transformation, and to remind you of the limitless strength you carry within. I hope it has stirred something profound in your spirit—a spark that encourages you to step boldly into your purpose.

Looking Back

Think about the challenges you've faced in life. Reflect on how far you've come despite those obstacles. Every setback, every struggle, and every moment of doubt has shaped you into the resilient woman you are today. Your journey matters and your story is powerful. Let it remind you of the strength that resides in you, even when circumstances feel overwhelming.

1. What has resonated with you most deeply from this book?

2. What past experiences can you now view through a lens of strength and growth?

3. What will it take for you to rise into the woman you were called to be?

Please visit DaughterAriseBook.com, and let us know what you think about the book.

Hopefully, this book has been a blessing to you. This organization, this platform, this ministry, this movement, was designed by God for women just like you. No matter what your walk of life is. No matter what your financial situation looks like. You are a woman, and if you have initiated a relationship with God, you are a woman of God, who has purpose and destiny. My desire is simply to encourage you. Inspire you. Uplift you. And do whatever I can do to help you arise.

www.ingramcontent.com/pod-product-compliance
Lightning Source LLC
LaVergne TN
LVHW051154080426
835508LV00021B/2614